# From Root to Plate

DAWNA DRAKE

From Root to Plate
Copyright © 2021 by Dawna Drake
Cover Photo: Grayson Birch
Cover Photo Art and Graphics: Dawna Drake

All rights reserved. No part of this publication may be reproduced, distributed, or transmitted in any form or by any means, including photocopying, recording, or other electronic or mechanical methods, without the prior written permission of the author, except in the case of brief quotations embodied in critical reviews and certain other non-commercial uses permitted by copyright law.

Tellwell Talent
www.tellwell.ca

ISBN
978-0-9783603-1-3 (Paperback)

This book is for those who believed it was possible.
Thank you

# Table of Contents

sewn .................................................................................... 1
a sentence given ................................................................ 2
bare .................................................................................... 3
tread ................................................................................... 4
rising tide .......................................................................... 5
resonate ............................................................................. 6
the fall is near .................................................................. 7
a reminder stained .......................................................... 8
the game ............................................................................ 9
happy ............................................................................... 10
hurt .................................................................................. 10
a session with Mr. paper and Dr. pen ........................ 11
move ................................................................................ 12
aging ................................................................................ 13
carved .............................................................................. 14
child's pieces .................................................................. 15
offered ............................................................................. 16
cage .................................................................................. 17
trust ................................................................................. 18
unexpected ..................................................................... 19
from root to plate ......................................................... 20
lullaby .............................................................................. 21
suddenly ......................................................................... 22
frayed .............................................................................. 23
we could play in the mud ............................................ 24
knavery ........................................................................... 25
the alter .......................................................................... 26

| | |
|---|---|
| crumbs | 27 |
| form of me | 28 |
| untapped | 29 |
| desperation | 30 |
| a shot away | 31 |
| what they could not parry | 32 |
| corduroy beat | 33 |
| a tone meant | 34 |
| unspoken words | 35 |
| hold you, still | 36 |
| supposed psalm | 37 |
| years | 38 |
| it's a shame | 39 |

## sewn

happier you'd be
perhaps if I were made of
altered stitchery
frayed pieces of someone else
woven neatly onto me

# a sentence given

it's a moment
it's an hour
afflicted with a pale stranger's loneliness
a day
a week
a hunger comes calling to fill the openness
a month
a year
disillusioned by the faces that have passed
it's a distance
it's an eternity
a sentence given for an unforgiven past

# bare

stripped bare I crouch and contemplate
why destiny would crack my fate
this corner can't conceal my dirt
nor can it comprehend this hurt
shamed, I wish to consecrate
but I can't seem to desecrate
all these things I've grown to hate
my skin unbuttons like a shirt
stripped bare, I crouch

you never could appreciate
the agony inside the wait
conjuring up a fragile flirt
knowing I would never convert
my exposed bones won't hesitate
stripped bare, I crouch

## tread

where the shadow of what was
lays a tread from the
heavy boot of time
still
inside the daylight
wears a happy limb
of the tree we could not climb

# rising tide

these aren't tired eyes
they're broken moments
and lost hope
bricks tied to my lashes
these aren't tears
they're dew drops
from my beating heart,
a rising tide
of broken trust

# resonate

rain on the chamber resonates
tender moments hidden in the mist
a jealous field of lilies complain
love is not love if it hesitates
with a smile wrapped in a fist
rain on the chamber resonates
that crimson memory tryst
of candy and crowns; a cerulean stain
tender moments hidden in the mist
the verdant hemline of night arrives again
to settle hips that contemplate
rain on the chamber resonates
tender moments hidden in the mist
a jealous field of lilies complain

# the fall is near

the fall is near
I can feel it
the chill in the air
hinders the applause
by the gentle breeze,
it's shedding season
limbs exposed so the truth
is not long hidden
I am barely a leaf
on the tree of your life
and the fall is near
I can feel it

# a reminder stained

I have been here before
I did not enjoy my stay
I lost my head, my voice
and most of me along the way

these roots on which I carved
like a slave to this cause
so many layers sliced and exposed
I forgot who I was

like a fairy in the autumn leaves
crushed under the pile
a reminder stained under my wings
that my last stay was too long a while

# the game

I'm tortured when you're with me
but you haunt me when you go
it's the way you play the game
I'm the game, I know

pawns and knights
a hollow battle, quiet
an unarmed queen dies
too tired to riot

so, pick up your armor
steady your feet
the ghosts are coming
there will be no retreat

I'm haunted by this
never ending show
it's the way you play the game
I'm the game
I know

## happy

I forgot what happy looked like
until you
slapped it off my face

## hurt

peeling back the skin
to reveal the meat
underneath, my broken heart

# a session with Mr. paper and Dr. pen

I think I am bi-polar
how do I deduce
by my very supposition?
but let not my supposition deduce
that one must seek attention through
the device of such an issue
I certainly would not
but suppose I was right to deduce
not that I have thought to seduce
any repercussions

## move

I don't want to move
forward
   or onward
      or upward
with anyone -
I want to move
inward
because that is where
my soul lives

# aging

my wooden arms
sprout no beefy twigs
how could beauty become
from such rough things?

no smooth contours
or flawless lines
only dark patchy scabs
wrapped in veiny vines

my time thickened roots
have wrinkled under moss
muddy footprints seep into
where my well of life once was

these rings resolve to strangling
desiring to spread my grain
how does a beauty outgrow these knots
and learn to breathe again

## carved

it seems I've been dragging
this body of stone for so long
I have carved miles of shallow grave

determined to follow paper planes
in an interminable sky, all along
from my past my future waves

# child's pieces

amongst the flowers and the earth
I left my child's pieces
soiled with grief
and the fragrance of remembrance
deep within my memory's creases
with no casket, no stone
an unmarked grave lay within my heart

inside
out among the flowers
and the earth
I have left my child's pieces

# offered

lilies offered
a smile returned
for a brief collapse of humor
taciturn heart, a smear of guilt
stratified beneath
lilac whispers exchanged
inside patient sheets
and heavy wine

if only they were
offered another time

## cage

someone broke into
my bony cage
and tried to kill the beast
thrashing about
in some sort of rage
somehow it was released

## trust

take little steps, don't
rush the cliff, when the
urge to dive off overwhelms you
step back and watch the birds
trust in their own wings

## unexpected

there were stars once
like gleaming gems
back when I was
thankful for night

balancing on the teeth
of the unexpected
a bite reveals the truth
inside the dying light

those bursting hearts
an unexpected memory
that returns my mind
to that beautiful sight

# from root to plate

take me as I am, learn
me, inside out
hold all my demons close
for I alone will resuscitate
this home for ghosts
where reality is doubt
take me as I am, turn
me inside out
hold all of me close
say you will learn
me, from root to plate

# lullaby

inside my heart a garrulous noise
a swooning sparrow
a sotto voce eulogy underneath

the trim of each timorous verse
rippling through somber flesh
that soft sullen

lullaby
searching for your arms
your voice, your ashes

your oracular slink
seamlessly tucked under
wings of a swooning sparrow

# suddenly

in the shadow of what we knew
I heard a familiar break
as its laughter fervently grew
to release the patient light
suddenly I am awake
your comfort comes in subtle
hues, such a grateful sight
something beautiful from the muddle
gives our world a shake

# frayed

when our blue flesh gathers
rising in the soft whimper of day
these frayed seams become
a steady limb
my heart stands at attention
for moments like this

# we could play in the mud

we could play in the mud
you could make it delicious,
like a fresh chocolate cookie
smeared on my little freckled face
but the street-lights come on
and my mother's calling
the man is waking up

the closet seems smaller
now, these torn jeans could use a wash
the doorknob looks like a jewel
when the key turns in it,
sometimes the darkness
is the wisest thing I know
because I've known it the longest
still, the sun will argue

you smell like fresh laundry
and my nails are always dirty
with you even the rocks are fascinating
I would make them all pets for you
if only I could stay
we could play in the mud
you could make it delicious

# knavery

slowly between the rise
and set of day
a random moment of bravery
rebels within my heart
an emotional dismemberment
where the horizon starts
your lavish knavery
leaves creativity to play
just behind those dark eyes

# the alter

innocence at bible camp
that sweet smell of cedar
and a dying fire

you crushed me
into the springs
into the cross
into the wall
into the dirt floor
into the heaving moon
you changed
me

the morning still smoking
let the embers be
a beacon of truth

## crumbs

the sun grain through her dirty window
shades her personal internment
swirling hesitantly like cream
in day old coffee

a moment on the lips
of a salacious memory

his clothes
a trail of crumbs
to a place
she cannot return from

# form of me

it's hard to believe
too far gone to see
how is it I got here
without any form of me?

my mind shaken
like a childhood game
bits of me are in there
but I'll never look the same

## untapped

there's a light wrapped
tightly around this space
gleaming with words that bark
with fangs in the dark
smoke mirrors my face
my heart is still untapped

# desperation

it's not the grief of a child
that whines because you are gone
it's not the naïve matron
of love trying to hold on

it's not the fading memories
deceiving this precious time
it's only love of a human nature
that's stepping out of line

it's not the heart
of an animal pounding after death
it's not the smell of defeat
sewn on a soldier's breath

it's not the sweet bitterness
hidden deep within the nun
it's only desperation grasping
denying that it's done

# a shot away

It seems you know
what it is to have
an empty heart
how I envy you for that,

mine is
   heavy
with the plague
of this love
this brick
in my chest
and a gun in my throat
happiness is but
   a shot away

# what they could not parry

It was a crisp day
quiet morning fog of
lost Indian summer
un-buds roaring yellow
and orange screaming
the quiet    still    truth
thrusting through the
sun burnt grass
yet, bare limbed trees could
not conceal those eyes
from such a cold discovery
some battles are
not worth this scene

a graveyard made
in hasty marsh
beside these barren
paths where flocks sing
a sorrowful refrain
for the loneliness of this day
and what they could not parry
shedding season chill sets in
the same fists
that dented this dirt
stops our hearts
in truth, we must bury

November 5, 2008
(for Brandon Crisp)

## corduroy beat

listen to the footsteps
of my voice
it's how you'll hear
the corduroy beat
of my heart

listen to the shadows
of my memory
it's how you'll feel
the distance weep
while we're apart

# a tone meant

I should have known
that moment
I could not seize
the words that fell from his
broken lips and resonated
in this bony cage
around my galloping pulp
it was a tone meant
to open my ears
and shut my eyes
to his atonement
and my demise

## unspoken words

draped in deception
flowers wilting in the vase
with so many memories
dancing away these days

of looking through the truth
trying to build what's undesired
leftover broken trust and promises
our eyes growing tired

all these good intentions
unravel like the sun
wraps itself around our tender
branches until each leaf comes undone

it has no commitment; written
on wings of a blinded bird
that sings un-caged, aloud
for freedom and unspoken words

petal by petal we float along
the sullen river of forget,
one must seek to remember love is
to know one can and not regret

# hold you, still

alone on the deck
the dawn clawing
at the horizon
reflecting in the glass lake
a smile drifts in
with the rolling dew
and I am reminded
of the fall
and you
beside me

I hold you, still
only now
in a small red box
with a bronze clasp

## supposed psalm

there's a calm
where the fall should scream
if I could re-arrange
all of what this seems
to be
a garden in bloom
a violet awkward strange
desolate in between
of what is a supposed psalm

## years

that old chair, still nodding
to the empty dirt road
with post war hope
after all these years
if this porch could talk
tired peeling paint
offers the sunlit comfort
for all the tears
that tried to cope
without your conversation
waving flags as you rode
away; that old chair
still nodding

# it's a shame

it's the
shim sham
flip-flop flip
rim-rim-rim
of my bobblehead heart
rat-rat-rat rattlin'
off my frim fram cage
threatnin' a start
givin' a dim-dim damn
but it's a damn-damn-damn
shame
there ain't no
tickety rickety skip slip
other bobblehead worthy
of this frickety fracken
skippin' heart
a dim damn
shame

www.ingramcontent.com/pod-product-compliance
Lightning Source LLC
LaVergne TN
LVHW041552060526
838200LV00037B/1251